F1 LEGENDS ALPHABET

Words by Robin Feiner

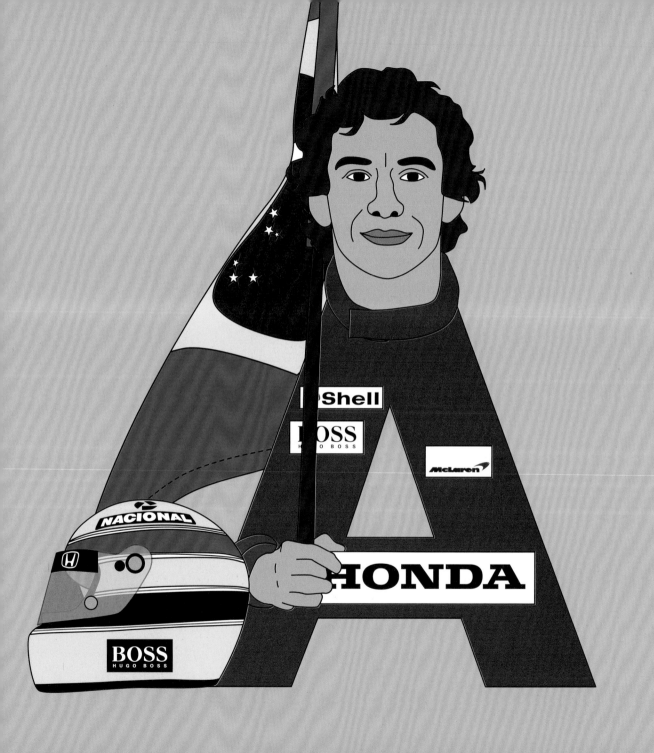

A is for **A**yrton Senna. A tragic crash in 1994 cut short the life of the most talented driver the world had ever seen. 'Magic Senna' won F1 World Championships in '88, '90, and '91, while his rivalry with fellow McLaren driver Alain Prost electrified the sport. This legend will forever live in the hearts of F1 fans.

B is for Jack Brabham. 'Black Jack' knew his way around a car—not just on the track but also in the auto body shop. The Aussie won three F1 World Championships during his legendary career, but he's most fondly remembered for being the only man to win in a car he built with his own bare hands.

C is for Jim **C**lark.
Some call Clark the most gifted driver ever to sit behind the steering wheel. In 1963, he led 71 percent of all the laps he raced in—still a record to this day. Many years after his fatal crash, fellow F1 legend Jackie Stewart described Clark as 'the best racing driver I ever raced against.'

D is for **D**avid Coulthard. Though he never won the 'big one' (he had Michael Schumacher to thank for that), the man with the incredible jawline did place in the top five of the F1 Championship seven times. DC finished with a total of 13 Grand Prix victories before retiring from F1 after the 2008 season.

E is for Enzo Ferrari.
What's in a name? Beauty. Innovation. Legend. Ferrari encapsulates all that and more. Enzo, who started as a Grand Prix driver in an Alfa, built his first car in 1937. Scuderia Ferrari went on to dominate the next century of F1— today, no team has won more Drivers' or Constructors' Championships.

F is for Fernando Alonso. This Spanish speed demon was an instant sensation, becoming the youngest driver ever to win the F1 World Championship with his 2005 victory for Renault (a record that's since been broken). Still racing, and now with two World Championships under his belt, he's one of the few true legends in the paddock.

G is for **G**raham Hill. Somehow, Hill didn't pass his driver's exam until he was 24. But from then on, he never stopped racing. He's still the only man to capture the legendary 'Triple Crown of Motorsport'—winning the Indy 500, the 24 Hours of Le Mans, and the Monaco Grand Prix all in one year.

H is for Lewis Hamilton. 'The Billion Dollar Man' transcends F1. He's racked up 103 checkered flags, 183 podium finishes, and 7 World Championships— all records (the latter shared with Schumi). He's also the first and only Black driver ever to win an F1 race. Lewis is the GOAT. What more is there to say?

JACKY ICKX

Ii

I is for Jacky Ickx.
If nothing else, Ickx was tough. After suffering severe burns in a devasting 1970 car crash, this legend returned to racing just 17 days later at the Monaco Grand Prix. He won eight F1 races (and an astonishing six 24 Hours of Le Mans) while driving for Ferrari, Brabham, and Lotus.

J is for Juan Manuel Fangio. This agile Argentinian dominated F1 during the '50s, winning 24 Grands Prix and 5 World Championships while racing for the likes of Ferrari, Mercedes, and Maserati. Fangio was famous for winning races at the slowest possible speed— to preserve the life of each of his beloved cars.

K is for **K**imi Räikkönen. 'The Iceman' is the last driver to bring F1 glory to Ferrari, having won the World Championship in 2007. His brash personality has rubbed many the wrong way, but he's also fondly remembered for his playfulness—like eating an ice cream cone during a momentarily suspended race!

L is for Niki **L**auda.
The 1976 Nürburgring Crash:
when the world's best driver
caught fire and nearly lost his
life. Somehow, he came back
and continued his legendary
career. Lauda is still the only
F1 driver to have won World
Championships for the sport's
two most prestigious teams:
McLaren and Ferrari.

M is for Stirling **M**oss.
For a brief time, Sir Stirling Moss was famous for breaking the world speed record. And while Moss won many races, he's best known for being the greatest driver to have never won an F1 World Championship. Despite that, true fans of the sport will forever call him a legend.

Nn

N is for Nigel Mansell.
This legendary Brit had successful stints with the four premier names in F1 racing: McLaren, Ferrari, Lotus, and Williams. After finishing as runner-up on three separate occasions, Mansell finally captured racing's greatest title with his 1992 Formula One World Championship.

O is for Formula One.
Following WWII, the FIA
agreed on a set of rules that
constructors and drivers had
to follow, which they called
Formula One. The sport took
off shortly thereafter, and
today, F1 is the highest form
of open-wheel, single-seat
driving and the pinnacle
of motorsports.

P is for Alain **P**rost. Strategic, political, and debonair. 'The Professor's' rivalry with Ayrton Senna dominated the late '80s and early '90s era of F1, as the two combined for seven F1 World Championships in a nine-year stretch. His greatest days came while he was driving for McLaren.

Q is for Nelson Piquet Sr. Before Prost and Senna, there was Nelson Piquet. While staying busy winning three F1 World Championships, Piquet became known for his generous humor and his commitment to winning. He once said, 'I don't want to make friends with anybody who's important. I just want to win.'

Rr

R is for Nico Rosberg. There's no doubting Nico has the heart of a true champion. Capturing the 2016 World Championship for Mercedes in stunning fashion, he outmaneuvered Lewis Hamilton himself. Aside from being a legend behind the wheel, Nico is also lauded for his philanthropy and eco-entrepreneurial focus.

S is for Michael **S**chumacher. Four years old—that was Schumi's age when he first got behind the wheel. Is it any surprise he became the greatest? 'The Red Baron's' legendary career saw him win 91 races, 7 World Championships, and return Ferrari to glory. It would be hard to find a fiercer competitor in any sport.

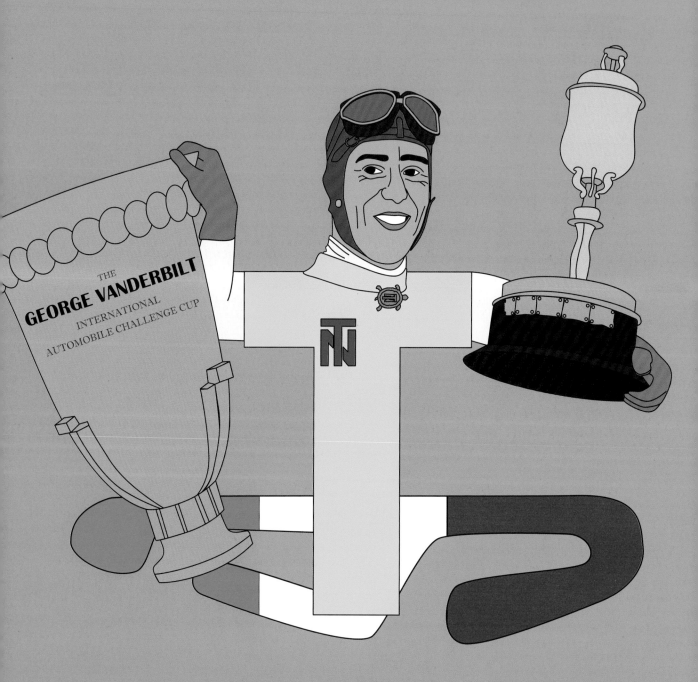

T is for **T**azio Nuvolari. Ferdinand Porsche once called Nuvolari 'the greatest driver of the past, the present, and the future.' And while Tazio's heyday may have come before F1 was fully formed, he still won a total of 24 Grands Prix and the 1932 Drivers' Championship—Legendary!

U is for James Hunt 'The Shunt.' Portrayed by Chris Hemsworth in the 2013 film Rush, Hunt was F1's most notorious bad boy. He earned his nickname, The Shunt, for his reckless driving abilities and fearless attitude. His style propelled him to a 1976 F1 World Championship while driving with McLaren.

V is for Sebastian **V**ettel. The youngest World Champion in F1 history has been a mainstay on the circuit since first bursting onto the scene in 2007, winning four World Championships with Red Bull. Vettel is also known for naming his cars—among the monikers are Luscious Liz, Kinky Kylie, and Hungry Heidi.

W is for Murray **W**alker. Sometimes, it's not the man behind the wheel, but the man behind the microphone who becomes a legend. In no sense is that truer than with renowned motorsport commentator Murray Walker. From '76 to '96, Walker called every race under the sun and became the voice of F1.

Xx

X is for **Max** Verstappen. And a legend is born before our very eyes. After a nail-biting and often controversial battle with Hamilton through-out the '21 season, Verstappen in the Red Bull miraculously came out on top! Now, the sky's the limit for the young Mad Max.

Y is for Sir John **Y**oung 'Jackie' Stewart. Britain's finest driver ever was none other than Sir Jackie. During his illustrious nine-year career racing for Tyrrell, 'The Flying Scot' dominated the F1 circuit. He easily won World Championships in 1969, 1971, and 1973, finishing at least 16 poll points ahead of the runner-up all three years.

WILLIAMS F1

DF1 DF1

Z

ELTI

Alex Zanardi

Z is for Alex Zanardi. While Zanardi's F1 career was respectable enough, what made him a true legend came in the aftermath of his 2001 crash at the EuroSpeedway Lausitz. Zanardi had both legs amputated—but that didn't stop him from returning to an F1 car in 2006 or from becoming an eventual Paralympic champion.

The ever-expanding legendary library

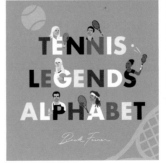

EXPLORE THESE LEGENDARY ALPHABETS & MORE AT WWW.ALPHABETLEGENDS.COM

F1 LEGENDS ALPHABET
www.alphabetlegends.com

Published by Alphabet Legends Pty Ltd in 2022
Created by Beck Feiner
Copyright © Alphabet Legends Pty Ltd 2022

Printed and bound in China.

9780645200188